This Astronomy Notebook

is the property of:

Date/Time:
Location/GPS:

For my observation, i used:

☐ My eyes ☐ Binoculars ☐ Telescope

The objects that i saw in the sky are :

☐ Moon   ☐ Planet   ☐ Galaxy

☐ Star   ☐ Constellation ☐ Comet

I'm happy to see this object (Draw me)

Moon Phase

☐ New Moon   ☐ Full Moon

☐ Waxing Crescent   ☐ Waning Gibbous

☐ First Quarter   ☐ Third Quarter

☐ Waxing Gibbous   ☐ Waning Crescent

(Mark me)   **(Mark me)**

My notes:

Date/Time:
Location/GPS:

For my observation, i used:

☐ My eyes ☐ Binoculars ☐ Telescope

The objects that i saw in the sky are :

☐ Moon ☐ Planet ☐ Galaxy

☐ Star ☐ Constellation ☐ Comet

I'm happy to see this object (Draw me)

Moon Phase

- [ ] New Moon
- [ ] Waxing Crescent
- [ ] First Quarter
- [ ] Waxing Gibbous

- [ ] Full Moon
- [ ] Waning Gibbous
- [ ] Third Quarter
- [ ] Waning Crescent

(Mark me)

(Mark me)

My notes:

Date/Time:
Location/GPS:

For my observation, i used:

☐ My eyes   ☐ Binoculars   ☐ Telescope

The objects that i saw in the sky are :

☐ Moon   ☐ Planet   ☐ Galaxy

☐ Star   ☐ Constellation ☐ Comet

I'm happy to see this object (Draw me)

Moon Phase

- [ ] New Moon
- [ ] Waxing Crescent
- [ ] First Quarter
- [ ] Waxing Gibbous

- [ ] Full Moon
- [ ] Waning Gibbous
- [ ] Third Quarter
- [ ] Waning Crescent

(Mark me)

(Mark me)

My notes:

Date/Time:
Location/GPS:

For my observation, i used:

☐ My eyes ☐ Binoculars ☐ Telescope

The objects that i saw in the sky are :

☐ Moon ☐ Planet ☐ Galaxy

☐ Star ☐ Constellation ☐ Comet

I'm happy to see this object (Draw me)

Moon Phase

- ☐ New Moon
- ☐ Waxing Crescent
- ☐ First Quarter
- ☐ Waxing Gibbous

- ☐ Full Moon
- ☐ Waning Gibbous
- ☐ Third Quarter
- ☐ Waning Crescent

(Mark me)

(Mark me)

My notes:

Date/Time:
Location/GPS:

For my observation, i used:

☐ My eyes ☐ Binoculars ☐ Telescope

The objects that i saw in the sky are :

☐ Moon ☐ Planet ☐ Galaxy

☐ Star ☐ Constellation ☐ Comet

I'm happy to see this object (Draw me)

Moon Phase

☐ New Moon   ☐ Full Moon

☐ Waxing Crescent   ☐ Waning Gibbous

☐ First Quarter   ☐ Third Quarter

☐ Waxing Gibbous   ☐ Waning Crescent

(Mark me)   **(Mark me)**

My notes:

Date/Time:
Location/GPS:

For my observation, i used:

☐ My eyes   ☐ Binoculars   ☐ Telescope

The objects that i saw in the sky are :

☐ Moon   ☐ Planet   ☐ Galaxy

☐ Star   ☐ Constellation ☐ Comet

I'm happy to see this object (Draw me)

Moon Phase

☐ New Moon

☐ Full Moon

☐ Waxing Crescent

☐ Waning Gibbous

☐ First Quarter

☐ Third Quarter

☐ Waxing Gibbous

☐ Waning Crescent

(Mark me)

(Mark me)

My notes:

Date/Time:
Location/GPS:

For my observation, i used:

☐ My eyes ☐ Binoculars ☐ Telescope

The objects that i saw in the sky are :

☐ Moon ☐ Planet ☐ Galaxy

☐ Star ☐ Constellation ☐ Comet

I'm happy to see this object (Draw me)

Moon Phase

- [ ] New Moon
- [ ] Waxing Crescent
- [ ] First Quarter
- [ ] Waxing Gibbous

- [ ] Full Moon
- [ ] Waning Gibbous
- [ ] Third Quarter
- [ ] Waning Crescent

(Mark me)

(Mark me)

My notes:

Date/Time:
Location/GPS:

For my observation, i used:

☐ My eyes ☐ Binoculars ☐ Telescope

The objects that i saw in the sky are :

☐ Moon   ☐ Planet   ☐ Galaxy

☐ Star   ☐ Constellation ☐ Comet

I'm happy to see this object (Draw me)

Moon Phase

☐ New Moon ☐ Full Moon

☐ Waxing Crescent ☐ Waning Gibbous

☐ First Quarter ☐ Third Quarter

☐ Waxing Gibbous ☐ Waning Crescent

(Mark me) **(Mark me)**

My notes:

Date/Time:
Location/GPS:

For my observation, i used:

☐ My eyes ☐ Binoculars ☐ Telescope

The objects that i saw in the sky are :

☐ Moon ☐ Planet ☐ Galaxy

☐ Star ☐ Constellation ☐ Comet

I'm happy to see this object (Draw me)

Moon Phase

- [ ] New Moon
- [ ] Waxing Crescent
- [ ] First Quarter
- [ ] Waxing Gibbous

- [ ] Full Moon
- [ ] Waning Gibbous
- [ ] Third Quarter
- [ ] Waning Crescent

(Mark me)

(Mark me)

My notes:

Date/Time:
Location/GPS:

For my observation, i used:

☐ My eyes   ☐ Binoculars   ☐ Telescope

The objects that i saw in the sky are :

☐ Moon   ☐ Planet   ☐ Galaxy

☐ Star   ☐ Constellation   ☐ Comet

I'm happy to see this object (Draw me)

Moon Phase

- [ ] New Moon
- [ ] Waxing Crescent
- [ ] First Quarter
- [ ] Waxing Gibbous

- [ ] Full Moon
- [ ] Waning Gibbous
- [ ] Third Quarter
- [ ] Waning Crescent

(Mark me)

(Mark me)

My notes:

Date/Time:
Location/GPS:

For my observation, i used:

☐ My eyes ☐ Binoculars ☐ Telescope

The objects that i saw in the sky are :

☐ Moon   ☐ Planet   ☐ Galaxy

☐ Star   ☐ Constellation ☐ Comet

I'm happy to see this object (Draw me)

Moon Phase

☐ New Moon   ☐ Full Moon

☐ Waxing Crescent   ☐ Waning Gibbous

☐ First Quarter   ☐ Third Quarter

☐ Waxing Gibbous   ☐ Waning Crescent

(Mark me)   **(Mark me)**

My notes:

Date/Time:
Location/GPS:

For my observation, i used:

☐ My eyes ☐ Binoculars ☐ Telescope

The objects that i saw in the sky are :

☐ Moon ☐ Planet ☐ Galaxy

☐ Star ☐ Constellation ☐ Comet

I'm happy to see this object (Draw me)

Moon Phase

☐ New Moon   ☐ Full Moon

☐ Waxing Crescent   ☐ Waning Gibbous

☐ First Quarter   ☐ Third Quarter

☐ Waxing Gibbous   ☐ Waning Crescent

(Mark me)   **(Mark me)**

My notes:

· ·
· ·
· ·
· ·
· ·
· ·
· ·
· ·
· ·
· ·
· ·

Date/Time:
Location/GPS:

For my observation, i used:

☐ My eyes   ☐ Binoculars   ☐ Telescope

The objects that i saw in the sky are :

☐ Moon   ☐ Planet   ☐ Galaxy

☐ Star   ☐ Constellation ☐ Comet

I'm happy to see this object (Draw me)

Moon Phase

- [ ] New Moon
- [ ] Waxing Crescent
- [ ] First Quarter
- [ ] Waxing Gibbous

- [ ] Full Moon
- [ ] Waning Gibbous
- [ ] Third Quarter
- [ ] Waning Crescent

(Mark me)

(Mark me)

My notes:

Date/Time:
Location/GPS:

For my observation, i used:

☐ My eyes ☐ Binoculars ☐ Telescope

The objects that i saw in the sky are :

☐ Moon ☐ Planet ☐ Galaxy

☐ Star ☐ Constellation ☐ Comet

I'm happy to see this object (Draw me)

Moon Phase

☐ New Moon   ☐ Full Moon

☐ Waxing Crescent   ☐ Waning Gibbous

☐ First Quarter   ☐ Third Quarter

☐ Waxing Gibbous   ☐ Waning Crescent

(Mark me)   **(Mark me)**

My notes:

Date/Time:
Location/GPS:

For my observation, i used:

☐ My eyes   ☐ Binoculars   ☐ Telescope

The objects that i saw in the sky are :

☐ Moon   ☐ Planet   ☐ Galaxy

☐ Star   ☐ Constellation   ☐ Comet

I'm happy to see this object (Draw me)

Moon Phase

- [ ] New Moon
- [ ] Waxing Crescent
- [ ] First Quarter
- [ ] Waxing Gibbous

- [ ] Full Moon
- [ ] Waning Gibbous
- [ ] Third Quarter
- [ ] Waning Crescent

(Mark me)

(Mark me)

My notes:

Date/Time:
Location/GPS:

For my observation, i used:

☐ My eyes ☐ Binoculars ☐ Telescope

The objects that i saw in the sky are :

☐ Moon ☐ Planet ☐ Galaxy

☐ Star ☐ Constellation ☐ Comet

I'm happy to see this object (Draw me)

Moon Phase

☐ New Moon   ☐ Full Moon

☐ Waxing Crescent   ☐ Waning Gibbous

☐ First Quarter   ☐ Third Quarter

☐ Waxing Gibbous   ☐ Waning Crescent

(Mark me)   **(Mark me)**

My notes:

Date/Time:
Location/GPS:

For my observation, i used:

☐ My eyes   ☐ Binoculars   ☐ Telescope

The objects that i saw in the sky are :

☐ Moon   ☐ Planet   ☐ Galaxy

☐ Star   ☐ Constellation ☐ Comet

I'm happy to see this object (Draw me)

Moon Phase

- [ ] New Moon
- [ ] Waxing Crescent
- [ ] First Quarter
- [ ] Waxing Gibbous

- [ ] Full Moon
- [ ] Waning Gibbous
- [ ] Third Quarter
- [ ] Waning Crescent

(Mark me)

(Mark me)

My notes:

Date/Time:
Location/GPS:

For my observation, i used:

☐ My eyes   ☐ Binoculars   ☐ Telescope

The objects that i saw in the sky are :

☐ Moon   ☐ Planet   ☐ Galaxy

☐ Star   ☐ Constellation ☐ Comet

I'm happy to see this object (Draw me)

Moon Phase

☐ New Moon   ☐ Full Moon

☐ Waxing Crescent   ☐ Waning Gibbous

☐ First Quarter   ☐ Third Quarter

☐ Waxing Gibbous   ☐ Waning Crescent

(Mark me)   **(Mark me)**

My notes:

Date/Time:
Location/GPS:

For my observation, i used:

☐ My eyes   ☐ Binoculars   ☐ Telescope

The objects that i saw in the sky are :

☐ Moon   ☐ Planet   ☐ Galaxy

☐ Star   ☐ Constellation   ☐ Comet

I'm happy to see this object (Draw me)

Moon Phase

☐ New Moon

☐ Waxing Crescent

☐ First Quarter

☐ Waxing Gibbous

☐ Full Moon

☐ Waning Gibbous

☐ Third Quarter

☐ Waning Crescent

(Mark me)

(Mark me)

My notes:

Date/Time:
Location/GPS:

For my observation, i used:

☐ My eyes ☐ Binoculars ☐ Telescope

The objects that i saw in the sky are :

☐ Moon ☐ Planet ☐ Galaxy

☐ Star ☐ Constellation ☐ Comet

I'm happy to see this object (Draw me)

Moon Phase

- [ ] New Moon
- [ ] Waxing Crescent
- [ ] First Quarter
- [ ] Waxing Gibbous

- [ ] Full Moon
- [ ] Waning Gibbous
- [ ] Third Quarter
- [ ] Waning Crescent

(Mark me)

(Mark me)

My notes:

· ·

· ·

· ·

· ·

· ·

· ·

· ·

· ·

· ·

· ·

· ·

Date/Time:
Location/GPS:

For my observation, i used:

☐ My eyes   ☐ Binoculars   ☐ Telescope

The objects that i saw in the sky are :

☐ Moon   ☐ Planet   ☐ Galaxy

☐ Star   ☐ Constellation   ☐ Comet

I'm happy to see this object (Draw me)

Moon Phase

- [ ] New Moon
- [ ] Waxing Crescent
- [ ] First Quarter
- [ ] Waxing Gibbous

- [ ] Full Moon
- [ ] Waning Gibbous
- [ ] Third Quarter
- [ ] Waning Crescent

(Mark me)

(Mark me)

My notes:

Date/Time:
Location/GPS:

For my observation, i used:

☐ My eyes ☐ Binoculars ☐ Telescope

The objects that i saw in the sky are :

☐ Moon ☐ Planet ☐ Galaxy

☐ Star ☐ Constellation ☐ Comet

I'm happy to see this object (Draw me)

Moon Phase

☐ New Moon   ☐ Full Moon

☐ Waxing Crescent   ☐ Waning Gibbous

☐ First Quarter   ☐ Third Quarter

☐ Waxing Gibbous   ☐ Waning Crescent

(Mark me)   **(Mark me)**

My notes:

Date/Time:
Location/GPS:

For my observation, i used:

☐ My eyes   ☐ Binoculars   ☐ Telescope

The objects that i saw in the sky are :

☐ Moon   ☐ Planet   ☐ Galaxy

☐ Star   ☐ Constellation   ☐ Comet

I'm happy to see this object (Draw me)

Moon Phase

☐ New Moon   ☐ Full Moon

☐ Waxing Crescent   ☐ Waning Gibbous

☐ First Quarter   ☐ Third Quarter

☐ Waxing Gibbous   ☐ Waning Crescent

(Mark me)   **(Mark me)**

My notes:

Date/Time:
Location/GPS:

For my observation, i used:

☐ My eyes ☐ Binoculars ☐ Telescope

The objects that i saw in the sky are :

☐ Moon ☐ Planet ☐ Galaxy

☐ Star ☐ Constellation ☐ Comet

I'm happy to see this object (Draw me)

Moon Phase

☐ New Moon ☐ Full Moon

☐ Waxing Crescent ☐ Waning Gibbous

☐ First Quarter ☐ Third Quarter

☐ Waxing Gibbous ☐ Waning Crescent

(Mark me) **(Mark me)**

My notes:

Date/Time:
Location/GPS:

For my observation, i used:

☐ My eyes ☐ Binoculars ☐ Telescope

The objects that i saw in the sky are :

☐ Moon ☐ Planet ☐ Galaxy

☐ Star ☐ Constellation ☐ Comet

I'm happy to see this object (Draw me)

Moon Phase

☐ New Moon   ☐ Full Moon

☐ Waxing Crescent   ☐ Waning Gibbous

☐ First Quarter   ☐ Third Quarter

☐ Waxing Gibbous   ☐ Waning Crescent

(Mark me)   **(Mark me)**

My notes:

Date/Time:
Location/GPS:

For my observation, i used:

☐ My eyes   ☐ Binoculars   ☐ Telescope

The objects that i saw in the sky are :

☐ Moon   ☐ Planet   ☐ Galaxy

☐ Star   ☐ Constellation   ☐ Comet

I'm happy to see this object (Draw me)

Moon Phase

- [ ] New Moon
- [ ] Waxing Crescent
- [ ] First Quarter
- [ ] Waxing Gibbous

- [ ] Full Moon
- [ ] Waning Gibbous
- [ ] Third Quarter
- [ ] Waning Crescent

(Mark me)

(Mark me)

My notes:

Date/Time:
Location/GPS:

For my observation, i used:

☐ My eyes   ☐ Binoculars   ☐ Telescope

The objects that i saw in the sky are :

☐ Moon   ☐ Planet   ☐ Galaxy

☐ Star   ☐ Constellation ☐ Comet

I'm happy to see this object (Draw me)

Moon Phase

☐ New Moon　　　　　　☐ Full Moon

☐ Waxing Crescent　　　☐ Waning Gibbous

☐ First Quarter　　　　　☐ Third Quarter

☐ Waxing Gibbous　　　☐ Waning Crescent

(Mark me)　　　　　　**(Mark me)**

My notes:

Date/Time:
Location/GPS:

For my observation, i used:

☐ **My eyes** ☐ **Binoculars** ☐ **Telescope**

The objects that i saw in the sky are :

☐ **Moon** ☐ **Planet** ☐ **Galaxy**

☐ **Star** ☐ **Constellation** ☐ **Comet**

I'm happy to see this object (Draw me)

Moon Phase

- [ ] New Moon
- [ ] Waxing Crescent
- [ ] First Quarter
- [ ] Waxing Gibbous

- [ ] Full Moon
- [ ] Waning Gibbous
- [ ] Third Quarter
- [ ] Waning Crescent

(Mark me)

(Mark me)

My notes:

Date/Time:
Location/GPS:

For my observation, i used:

☐ My eyes ☐ Binoculars ☐ Telescope

The objects that i saw in the sky are :

☐ Moon ☐ Planet ☐ Galaxy

☐ Star ☐ Constellation ☐ Comet

I'm happy to see this object (Draw me)

Moon Phase

- [ ] New Moon
- [ ] Waxing Crescent
- [ ] First Quarter
- [ ] Waxing Gibbous

- [ ] Full Moon
- [ ] Waning Gibbous
- [ ] Third Quarter
- [ ] Waning Crescent

(Mark me)

(Mark me)

My notes:

Date/Time:
Location/GPS:

For my observation, i used:

☐ My eyes ☐ Binoculars ☐ Telescope

The objects that i saw in the sky are :

☐ Moon ☐ Planet ☐ Galaxy

☐ Star ☐ Constellation ☐ Comet

I'm happy to see this object (Draw me)

Moon Phase

- [ ] New Moon
- [ ] Waxing Crescent
- [ ] First Quarter
- [ ] Waxing Gibbous

- [ ] Full Moon
- [ ] Waning Gibbous
- [ ] Third Quarter
- [ ] Waning Crescent

(Mark me)

(Mark me)

My notes:

Date/Time:
Location/GPS:

For my observation, i used:

☐ My eyes ☐ Binoculars ☐ Telescope

The objects that i saw in the sky are :

☐ Moon ☐ Planet ☐ Galaxy

☐ Star ☐ Constellation ☐ Comet

I'm happy to see this object (Draw me)

Moon Phase

- [ ] New Moon
- [ ] Waxing Crescent
- [ ] First Quarter
- [ ] Waxing Gibbous

- [ ] Full Moon
- [ ] Waning Gibbous
- [ ] Third Quarter
- [ ] Waning Crescent

(Mark me)

(Mark me)

My notes:

Date/Time:
Location/GPS:

For my observation, i used:

☐ My eyes ☐ Binoculars ☐ Telescope

The objects that i saw in the sky are :

☐ Moon ☐ Planet ☐ Galaxy

☐ Star ☐ Constellation ☐ Comet

I'm happy to see this object (Draw me)

Moon Phase

☐ New Moon   ☐ Full Moon

☐ Waxing Crescent   ☐ Waning Gibbous

☐ First Quarter   ☐ Third Quarter

☐ Waxing Gibbous   ☐ Waning Crescent

(Mark me)   **(Mark me)**

My notes:

Date/Time:
Location/GPS:

For my observation, i used:

☐ My eyes ☐ Binoculars ☐ Telescope

The objects that i saw in the sky are :

☐ Moon ☐ Planet ☐ Galaxy

☐ Star ☐ Constellation ☐ Comet

I'm happy to see this object (Draw me)

Moon Phase

☐ New Moon

☐ Waxing Crescent

☐ First Quarter

☐ Waxing Gibbous

☐ Full Moon

☐ Waning Gibbous

☐ Third Quarter

☐ Waning Crescent

(Mark me)

(Mark me)

My notes:

Date/Time:
Location/GPS:

For my observation, i used:

☐ My eyes ☐ Binoculars ☐ Telescope

The objects that i saw in the sky are :

☐ Moon ☐ Planet ☐ Galaxy

☐ Star ☐ Constellation ☐ Comet

I'm happy to see this object (Draw me)

Moon Phase

☐ New Moon   ☐ Full Moon

☐ Waxing Crescent   ☐ Waning Gibbous

☐ First Quarter   ☐ Third Quarter

☐ Waxing Gibbous   ☐ Waning Crescent

(Mark me)   **(Mark me)**

My notes:

Date/Time:
Location/GPS:

For my observation, i used:

☐ My eyes ☐ Binoculars ☐ Telescope

The objects that i saw in the sky are :

☐ Moon ☐ Planet ☐ Galaxy

☐ Star ☐ Constellation ☐ Comet

I'm happy to see this object (Draw me)

Moon Phase

- [ ] New Moon
- [ ] Waxing Crescent
- [ ] First Quarter
- [ ] Waxing Gibbous

- [ ] Full Moon
- [ ] Waning Gibbous
- [ ] Third Quarter
- [ ] Waning Crescent

(Mark me)

(Mark me)

My notes:

Date/Time:
Location/GPS:

For my observation, i used:

☐ My eyes ☐ Binoculars ☐ Telescope

The objects that i saw in the sky are :

☐ Moon ☐ Planet ☐ Galaxy

☐ Star ☐ Constellation ☐ Comet

I'm happy to see this object (Draw me)

Moon Phase

- [ ] New Moon
- [ ] Waxing Crescent
- [ ] First Quarter
- [ ] Waxing Gibbous

- [ ] Full Moon
- [ ] Waning Gibbous
- [ ] Third Quarter
- [ ] Waning Crescent

(Mark me)

(Mark me)

My notes:

Date/Time:
Location/GPS:

For my observation, i used:

☐ My eyes ☐ Binoculars ☐ Telescope

The objects that i saw in the sky are :

☐ Moon ☐ Planet ☐ Galaxy

☐ Star ☐ Constellation ☐ Comet

I'm happy to see this object (Draw me)

Moon Phase

- [ ] New Moon
- [ ] Waxing Crescent
- [ ] First Quarter
- [ ] Waxing Gibbous

- [ ] Full Moon
- [ ] Waning Gibbous
- [ ] Third Quarter
- [ ] Waning Crescent

(Mark me)

(Mark me)

My notes:

Date/Time:
Location/GPS:

For my observation, i used:

☐ My eyes ☐ Binoculars ☐ Telescope

The objects that i saw in the sky are :

☐ Moon ☐ Planet ☐ Galaxy

☐ Star ☐ Constellation ☐ Comet

I'm happy to see this object (Draw me)

Moon Phase

☐ New Moon

☐ Waxing Crescent

☐ First Quarter

☐ Waxing Gibbous

☐ Full Moon

☐ Waning Gibbous

☐ Third Quarter

☐ Waning Crescent

(Mark me)

(Mark me)

My notes:

Date/Time:
Location/GPS:

For my observation, i used:

☐ My eyes   ☐ Binoculars   ☐ Telescope

The objects that i saw in the sky are :

☐ Moon   ☐ Planet   ☐ Galaxy

☐ Star   ☐ Constellation ☐ Comet

I'm happy to see this object (Draw me)

Moon Phase

- [ ] New Moon
- [ ] Waxing Crescent
- [ ] First Quarter
- [ ] Waxing Gibbous

- [ ] Full Moon
- [ ] Waning Gibbous
- [ ] Third Quarter
- [ ] Waning Crescent

(Mark me)

(Mark me)

My notes:

Date/Time:
Location/GPS:

For my observation, i used:

☐ My eyes ☐ Binoculars ☐ Telescope

The objects that i saw in the sky are :

☐ Moon ☐ Planet ☐ Galaxy

☐ Star ☐ Constellation ☐ Comet

I'm happy to see this object (Draw me)

Moon Phase

☐ New Moon

☐ Waxing Crescent

☐ First Quarter

☐ Waxing Gibbous

☐ Full Moon

☐ Waning Gibbous

☐ Third Quarter

☐ Waning Crescent

(Mark me)

(Mark me)

My notes:

Date/Time:
Location/GPS:

For my observation, i used:

☐ My eyes ☐ Binoculars ☐ Telescope

The objects that i saw in the sky are :

☐ Moon ☐ Planet ☐ Galaxy

☐ Star ☐ Constellation ☐ Comet

I'm happy to see this object (Draw me)

Moon Phase

☐ New Moon

☐ Waxing Crescent

☐ First Quarter

☐ Waxing Gibbous

(Mark me)

☐ Full Moon

☐ Waning Gibbous

☐ Third Quarter

☐ Waning Crescent

(Mark me)

My notes:

Date/Time:
Location/GPS:

For my observation, i used:

☐ My eyes ☐ Binoculars ☐ Telescope

The objects that i saw in the sky are :

☐ Moon ☐ Planet ☐ Galaxy

☐ Star ☐ Constellation ☐ Comet

I'm happy to see this object (Draw me)

Moon Phase

- [ ] New Moon
- [ ] Waxing Crescent
- [ ] First Quarter
- [ ] Waxing Gibbous

- [ ] Full Moon
- [ ] Waning Gibbous
- [ ] Third Quarter
- [ ] Waning Crescent

(Mark me)

(Mark me)

My notes:

Date/Time:
Location/GPS:

For my observation, i used:

☐ My eyes   ☐ Binoculars   ☐ Telescope

The objects that i saw in the sky are :

☐ Moon   ☐ Planet   ☐ Galaxy

☐ Star   ☐ Constellation ☐ Comet

I'm happy to see this object (Draw me)

Moon Phase

- [ ] New Moon
- [ ] Waxing Crescent
- [ ] First Quarter
- [ ] Waxing Gibbous

- [ ] Full Moon
- [ ] Waning Gibbous
- [ ] Third Quarter
- [ ] Waning Crescent

(Mark me)

(Mark me)

My notes:

Date/Time:
Location/GPS:

For my observation, i used:

☐ My eyes ☐ Binoculars ☐ Telescope

The objects that i saw in the sky are :

☐ Moon ☐ Planet ☐ Galaxy

☐ Star ☐ Constellation ☐ Comet

I'm happy to see this object (Draw me)

Moon Phase

- [ ] New Moon
- [ ] Waxing Crescent
- [ ] First Quarter
- [ ] Waxing Gibbous

- [ ] Full Moon
- [ ] Waning Gibbous
- [ ] Third Quarter
- [ ] Waning Crescent

(Mark me)

(Mark me)

My notes:

Date/Time:
Location/GPS:

For my observation, i used:

☐ My eyes ☐ Binoculars ☐ Telescope

The objects that i saw in the sky are :

☐ Moon ☐ Planet ☐ Galaxy

☐ Star ☐ Constellation ☐ Comet

I'm happy to see this object (Draw me)

Moon Phase

☐ New Moon   ☐ Full Moon

☐ Waxing Crescent   ☐ Waning Gibbous

☐ First Quarter   ☐ Third Quarter

☐ Waxing Gibbous   ☐ Waning Crescent

(Mark me)   **(Mark me)**

My notes:

Date/Time:
Location/GPS:

For my observation, i used:

☐ My eyes ☐ Binoculars ☐ Telescope

The objects that i saw in the sky are :

☐ Moon ☐ Planet ☐ Galaxy

☐ Star ☐ Constellation ☐ Comet

I'm happy to see this object (Draw me)

Moon Phase

- [ ] New Moon
- [ ] Waxing Crescent
- [ ] First Quarter
- [ ] Waxing Gibbous

- [ ] Full Moon
- [ ] Waning Gibbous
- [ ] Third Quarter
- [ ] Waning Crescent

(Mark me)

(Mark me)

My notes:

Date/Time:
Location/GPS:

For my observation, i used:

☐ My eyes ☐ Binoculars ☐ Telescope

The objects that i saw in the sky are :

☐ Moon ☐ Planet ☐ Galaxy

☐ Star ☐ Constellation ☐ Comet

I'm happy to see this object (Draw me)

Moon Phase

- ☐ New Moon
- ☐ Waxing Crescent
- ☐ First Quarter
- ☐ Waxing Gibbous

- ☐ Full Moon
- ☐ Waning Gibbous
- ☐ Third Quarter
- ☐ Waning Crescent

(Mark me)

(Mark me)

My notes:

Date/Time:
Location/GPS:

For my observation, i used:

☐ My eyes   ☐ Binoculars   ☐ Telescope

The objects that i saw in the sky are :

☐ Moon   ☐ Planet   ☐ Galaxy

☐ Star   ☐ Constellation ☐ Comet

I'm happy to see this object (Draw me)

Moon Phase

☐ New Moon   ☐ Full Moon

☐ Waxing Crescent   ☐ Waning Gibbous

☐ First Quarter   ☐ Third Quarter

☐ Waxing Gibbous   ☐ Waning Crescent

(Mark me)   **(Mark me)**

My notes:

Date/Time:
Location/GPS:

For my observation, i used:

☐ **My eyes** ☐ **Binoculars** ☐ **Telescope**

The objects that i saw in the sky are :

☐ **Moon** ☐ **Planet** ☐ **Galaxy**

☐ **Star** ☐ **Constellation** ☐ **Comet**

I'm happy to see this object (Draw me)

Moon Phase

☐ New Moon

☐ Waxing Crescent

☐ First Quarter

☐ Waxing Gibbous

(Mark me)

☐ Full Moon

☐ Waning Gibbous

☐ Third Quarter

☐ Waning Crescent

(Mark me)

My notes:

Date/Time:
Location/GPS:

For my observation, i used:

☐ My eyes ☐ Binoculars ☐ Telescope

The objects that i saw in the sky are :

☐ Moon ☐ Planet ☐ Galaxy

☐ Star ☐ Constellation ☐ Comet

I'm happy to see this object (Draw me)

Moon Phase

☐ New Moon

☐ Waxing Crescent

☐ First Quarter

☐ Waxing Gibbous

☐ Full Moon

☐ Waning Gibbous

☐ Third Quarter

☐ Waning Crescent

(Mark me)

(Mark me)

My notes:

Printed in Great Britain
by Amazon